WORLD WAR II
Lost Words

COLIN HYNSON

KEY TO IMPORTANT ARTICLES

Look out for the following symbols through this book, highlighting key articles from the past.

FILM EXCERPT
Primary source material taken from a film about the subject matter.

SONG EXCERPT
Lyrics extracted from songs about the subject matter.

OFFICIAL SPEECH
Transcribed words from official government speeches.

GOVERNMENT DOCUMENT
Text extracted from an official government document.

LETTER
Text taken from a letter written by a participant in the events.

PLAQUE/INSCRIPTION
Text taken from plaques/monuments erected to remember momentous events described in this book.

INTERVIEW/BOOK EXTRACT
Text from an interview/book by somebody there at the time.

NEWSPAPER ARTICLE
Extracts taken from newspapers of the period.

TELEGRAM
Text taken from a telegram sent to or by a participant in the events.

An Hachette UK Company
www.hachette.co.uk

First published in Great Britain in 2005 by TickTock, a division of Octopus Publishing Group Ltd,
Endeavour House, 189 Shaftesbury Avenue, London, WC2H 8JY.
www.octopusbooks.co.uk

Copyright © Octopus Publishing Group Ltd 2012

ISBN 978 1 84898 696 1

A CIP catalogue record for this book is available from the British Library

Printed in Hong Kong
10 9 8 7 6 5 4

CONTENTS

INTRODUCTION

Above *These German stamps were issued in the 1930s and depict the face of the country's dictator, Adolf Hitler. Hitler was responsible for plunging the world into war.*

Below *During World War II the British Army was supplemented by the Home Guard, like these men from Treeton, England.*

Between the years 1939 and 1945 the world was gripped by the largest and most destructive war in human history. Never before had so many people – both military and civilian – been caught up in the horrors of warfare. The suffering caused by the war was felt in nearly every country on the planet. This six-year conflict ended with the complete destruction of two cities using a terrible new weapon that would cast a shadow over the world right up until the present day. The end of the Second World War also saw the rise of the Soviet Union and the United States of America as the two world superpowers.

The main reason for the start of the Second World War can be traced back to the end of the First World War in 1918. Germany, Italy and Japan all came out of the First World War resentful about the way that the Allied

Forces of France, Britain and the United States had treated them. This despite the fact that during World War I both Italy and Japan were on the victorious side. This resentment eventually led to the rise of governments that were determined to make up for what they believed they had lost in 1918. Germany and Italy had dictatorships, and in Japan the military kept a firm grip on the civilian government. The Second World War started on the morning of September 1, 1939 when the German army invaded Poland.

Above Allied soldiers ready for action during 1943.

Left Though aircraft had been used in World War I, air power was used to an unprecedented extent during the Second World War.

Below As men went to war, women were recruited to do their work. "Land Girls" in their distinctive uniform were a familiar sight on Britain's farms.

Two days later Britain and France declared war on Germany. By the summer of 1940 the Germans and their Italian allies controlled much of Europe. On June 22, 1941, the war spread even further when the Germans invaded the Soviet Union.

The war so far was confined to Europe and to some limited battles in North Africa. On December 7, 1941 the war truly turned into a global conflict when the Japanese attacked the American Pacific Fleet at Pearl Harbour. The war was now being fought in Asia and the Pacific. When Germany and Italy declared war on the United States on December 11, 1941, the conflict now stretched across the world. At first the Germans, Italians and Japanese, (the so-called Axis Powers) did well. France had fallen and Britain faced Germany alone. The attack on the Soviet Union was swift, and by

Above *Provisions were limited during the war, with everyday items such as tea subject to rationing.*

Below *Field Marshal Erwin Rommel fought in World War I and came to prominence as a skilled general in World War II.*

the end of December 1941, the German army was approaching Moscow. In Asia and the Pacific the Japanese conquered Bursa, Hong Kong, the Philippines and Singapore and seemed to threaten both India and Australia.

It was not until the Summer and Autumn of 1942 that the tide began to turn with the American victory at Midway on 4 June and the British success at El Alamein in late October. The key turning point however came in February 1943 with the German surrender at Stalingrad. Helped by the cold Russian winter, the Germans were slowly pushed back out of the Soviet Union. In June 1942, the Japanese advance was

Above *A scene from the film Saving Private Ryan, set in World War II. The movie offers one of the most realistic portrayals ever of what the violence of the war was really like.*

halted at the Battle of Midway. By the end of 1942 the Axis Powers were rapidly losing the territory that they had gained. One of the reasons for this was that they could not match the military and industrial strength of the Soviet Union and the United States. On June 6, 1944, Allied troops landed on the beaches of France. The Germans now found that they were fighting their enemies on two fronts. The end was inevitable. On May 8, 1945 the Germans surrendered and control was divided between France, Britain, the United States and the Soviet Union. In Asia and the Pacific the Japanese were slowly being pushed back. The Americans began "island-hopping". This meant taking back islands in the Pacific, so that eventually American bombers could attack the Japanese mainland. In November 1944, heavy air attacks on Japanese cities began. This culminated in the dropping of atomic bombs on Hiroshima and Nagasaki in August 1945. The Japanese surrendered informally on August 14, 1945 (formally on September 2) and World War II came to an end.

The world in 1945 was very different from the one that had existed in 1939. The British and the French now found themselves beginning to lose the power and influence that they used to hold, and the empires that they each held began to fall apart. Countries in Eastern Europe came under the control of the Soviet Union. China collapsed into a civil war that resulted in victory for the communists. The United States emerged from the war almost untouched, and grew into a global power. This led to the start of the Cold War between the Americans and the Soviet Union, that lasted until the 1980s. Today, this conflict has faded and relationships between east and west have improved, while other factors such as the fear of international terrorism in the wake of the World Trade Center attacks have seized centre stage.

Above A statue of Brigadier James Hill, one of the many heroes of the D-Day landing that helped bring an end to World War II.

Below The devastation caused by the dropping of an atomic bomb on the Japanese city of Hiroshima. The bombing effectively ended the war.

EARLY HISTORY A VICTIMISED GERMANY

Above *World War I was remembered by only one medal in the US, taking the form of the medal common to all the victorious allied nations.*

"In spite of such monstrous demands the rebuilding of our economic system is at the same time made impossible. We are to surrender our merchant fleet. We are to give up all foreign interests. We are to transfer to our opponents the property of all German undertakings abroad, even of those situated in countries allied to us. Even after the conclusion of peace the enemy states are to be empowered to confiscate all German property. No German merchant will then, in their countries, be safe from such war measures. We are to completely renounce our colonies… We are, in other words, to renounce every kind of political, economic and moral activity."

A view of the Treaty of Versailles by the German Foreign Minister who had to sign the treaty on behalf on Germany in 1919.

The origins of the Second World War can be traced back to mistakes made at the end of the First World War fought between Britain, France, Russia, Italy and the United States on one side and Germany, Austria-Hungary, Turkey and Bulgaria on the other. The war started in July 1914 and ended in November 1918 with the defeat of Germany and its allies. The grievances of whole nations combined with the hardships of economic depression to create aggressive governments determined to win back what they thought was rightfully theirs.

THE END OF THE FIRST WORLD WAR

Representatives from the victorious countries met at the Palace of Versailles near Paris in January 1919 to discuss the peace treaty with Germany. The Germans were not invited to take part in these discussions. However, they had to sign the final treaty when it was signed in June 1919. Under the terms of the Treaty, Germany had to reduce the size of its armed forces drastically. The army was cut to just 100,000 men and was not allowed on to German land to the left of the River Rhine. The once large and proud German Navy was reduced to just 24 ships.

Left *A sharecropper from Virginia in the United States. The Great Depression hit every part of the economy hard, from big business to farming.*

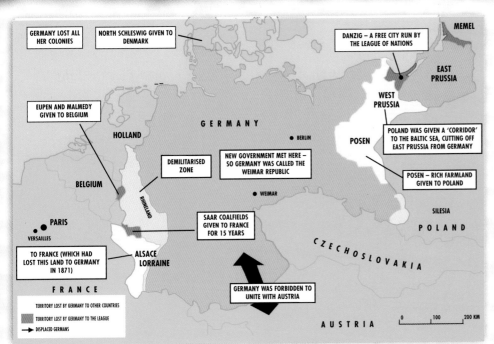

Labels on map:
- GERMANY LOST ALL HER COLONIES
- NORTH SCHLESWIG GIVEN TO DENMARK
- DANZIG – A FREE CITY RUN BY THE LEAGUE OF NATIONS
- MEMEL
- EAST PRUSSIA
- WEST PRUSSIA
- EUPEN AND MALMEDY GIVEN TO BELGIUM
- GERMANY
- HOLLAND
- BERLIN
- POSEN
- POLAND WAS GIVEN A 'CORRIDOR' TO THE BALTIC SEA, CUTTING OFF EAST PRUSSIA FROM GERMANY
- DEMILITARISED ZONE
- NEW GOVERNMENT MET HERE – SO GERMANY WAS CALLED THE WEIMAR REPUBLIC
- BELGIUM
- RHINELAND
- WEIMAR
- POSEN – RICH FARMLAND GIVEN TO POLAND
- PARIS
- VERSAILLES
- SAAR COALFIELDS GIVEN TO FRANCE FOR 15 YEARS
- SILESIA
- POLAND
- TO FRANCE (WHICH HAD LOST THIS LAND TO GERMANY IN 1871)
- ALSACE LORRAINE
- CZECHOSLOVAKIA
- FRANCE
- GERMANY WAS FORBIDDEN TO UNITE WITH AUSTRIA
- AUSTRIA
- 0   100   200 KM

Legend:
- TERRITORY LOST BY GERMANY TO OTHER COUNTRIES
- TERRITORY LOST BY GERMANY TO THE LEAGUE
- DISPLACED GERMANS

Above A map showing the territory lost by Germany as a result of the Treaty of Versailles.

TIMELINE
1918-1929

NOV 11, 1918
World War One Armistice signed at Compiègne, France.

JUNE 28, 1919
Treaty of Versailles signed.

JAN 3, 1925
Mussolini dismisses Italian parliament and becomes dictator.

OCT 29, 1929
Wall Street Stock Market crashes.

Below The Treaty of Versailles was signed in the famous Hall of Mirrors in the Palace of Versailles.

They were not allowed to have an air force of any kind. On top of that, the Germans lost land to countries that bordered it. All of their colonies in Africa and Asia were taken away. The Germans also had to pay for the damage caused by the war in Europe. This amounted to the equivalent of about $1.5 billion. The Treaty of Versailles was designed to make sure that Germany would never be a military threat in Europe again. However, the German people felt angry and humiliated by the Treaty. They thought that they had been treated unfairly and that the victorious powers were only interested in revenge.

THE GREAT DEPRESSION

In October 1929 the world began the slide into the "Great Depression". From 1929 to the middle of the 1930s the world suffered a huge economic downturn. Trade between nations collapsed. Thousands of companies went out of business. This meant that unemployment

"Sometimes during the winter… when the snow fell in Detroit they called for people that they wanted to shovel the snow, and of course everybody didn't get hired – you just had to go out there and the foreman or whoever would be throwing the shovel and if you happened to catch it you're hired. And so my father would go out there and on occasion he would be hired and earn a couple of dollars or so for the day's work there.

Shoes, of course, were a problem and many times I remember I wore out the soles down to the pavement, so to speak, and you had to put cardboard in there."

Memories of Richard Waskin, who was four when the Great Depression hit America in 1929.

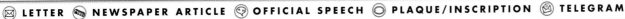

Above *The Germany army march into Poland during 1939.*

not only to work for the people but also to make their countries strong again. This meant that holding on to peace would be even more difficult.

THE FAILURE OF DEMOCRACY

For many people democratic governments had failed. The Treaty of Versailles had humiliated the Germans. Italy and Japan had fought on the victorious side but the Treaty appeared to give them very little. Many believed that firm and strong governments were needed to solve the crisis caused by the Depression. They saw democratic governments as weak and unable to take tough decisions.

Between 1919 and 1922 Italy had five different governments. There were street fights between the Communists and a new political force called the Fascists. In October

and poverty grew in many countries. Fourteen million people in the United States were unemployed, and three million people in Britain were also looking for work. More than six million people in Germany lost their jobs. In Japan, half the factories closed. In many of the countries that were badly hit by the Depression, people began to look towards political leaders who promised them jobs and stability. In Germany, Italy and Japan new governments came to power promising

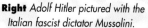

Right *Adolf Hitler pictured with the Italian fascist dictator Mussolini.*

"When we got in Hitler's speech was in progress on the radio and the Cowells were listening in. By missing some supper I managed to hear most of it, although I only understood a word of it here and there. The Führer was arresting and theatrical making the most of an emotional delivery. From what I could gather in fragments from the Cowells, he means no surrender. Sooner or later he will have Czechoslovakia; his armament and defences will be ready before the autumn is out. In each pause a crowd of thousands cheered and roared and howled. Hearing Hitler's very words and those frenzied howls brought home without doubt the terrible significance of it. Hitler means war."

The diary of Moyra Charlton from September 12, 1938. She later served with the British army as an ambulance driver.

Above *A row of wrecked buildings in Boundary Road, Shanghai during the Sino-Japanese War.*

NOV 8, 1931
Franklin Delano Roosevelt elected President of the United States.

JAN 30, 1933
Hitler appointed Chancellor of Germany.

JULY 14, 1933
Nazi party declared the official party of Germany.

Below *A map showing the territory of Manchuria, invaded by Japan in 1931.*

1922 the Fascist leader, Benito Mussolini, demanded that they should became the new Italian government. Faced by the possibility of civil war, this was accepted. Between 1924 and 1926 Mussolini made himself the dictator of Italy. Mussolini had an aggressive foreign policy and invaded Ethiopia in 1935 as the start of a new "Roman Empire".

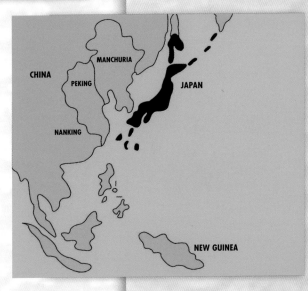

"For three months I had managed to avoid saluting the swastika flag... I tried it once too often, however... I caught sight of an approaching procession of Nazi nurses, carrying banners. Without stopping to think, I turned my back on it and walked in the opposite direction, only to face four Brownshirts crossing towards me from the other side of the street.

'Trying to get out of it?' said one. 'Arm up! And now?'

'Heil Hitler', I said.

I could have spat at myself as I strode past the procession with arm uplifted."

From **All Quiet in Germany** *by Karl Billinger, published in 1935.*

"During numerous raids today the German airmen have dropped thousands of articles of various kinds, including packets of food and sweets. The population have been warned not to touch any of these things. During one of the afternoon raids the German bombers scattered Polish banknotes in large quantities; these were discovered to be forgeries...

The effects of yesterday's raids have proved worse than had been expected. Everywhere buildings are lying in ruins. The Hospital of the Transfiguration was set on fire... Five doctors and several Red Cross nurses lost their lives. An emergency hospital is also in flames."

Stanislaw Balinski, a Polish journalist, witnessed the bombing of Warsaw in 1939.

EXPANSION IN JAPAN AND GERMANY

At the end of the First World War the Japanese had been given some land that had been controlled by the Germans. However, the Japanese felt that they should have been given more. The Depression also caused a lot of suffering in Japan. People in the armed forces blamed the "weakness" of their democratic government, and believed the solution was to conquer foreign lands. This would give Japanese factories the raw materials they needed, as well as a market to sell them. In September 1931 the Japanese army invaded a part of China called Manchuria. Back in Japan, the army began to control the government. Germany was very badly affected by the Depression. This helped the rise of a new political party called the National Socialists (or Nazis) under Adolf Hitler. The Nazi Party gained more power in the 1930s. In 1933

Hitler became the head of the German government and soon became dictator. He then began to build up Germany's armed forces. He believed that Germany needed more space, and began to take over lands around him. In 1938 he forced Austria to merge with Germany. He took Czechoslovakia in March 1939 and then turned his attention to Poland.

WAR BEGINS

The war in Europe began on the morning of September 1, 1939 when German forces crossed the eastern border of Germany and attacked Poland. This invasion had been expected for some time. After the Germans took over Czechoslovakia, the British and French governments had promised to come to the aid of Poland if it was next. Hitler did not believe that they would keep the promise. The attack on Poland introduced the world to a new type of warfare. This was called "blitzkrieg" or "lightning war". German tanks and planes smashed Polish defences, and the army moved swiftly through Poland. It was close to the Polish capital of Warsaw within a week.

Left *Adolf Hitler receives bouquets from three boys in the newly-merged Austria during a visit in 1940.*

 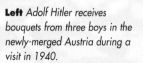

Above Crowds waiting outside Shanghai's City Hall to welcome China's General Chiang Kai-Shek on his return for the first time since the Japanese occupation of 1937.

POLAND DEFENDED

The British and French governments kept their promise. They demanded that Germany withdraw from Poland. Hitler did not respond. On September 3, they declared war on Germany. It was too late to save Poland. Hitler's Germany and the Soviet Union under Stalin had made a secret deal not to attack each other. On September 17, the Soviet army marched across its western border and attacked Poland. By September 20, all Poland was either in German or Soviet hands.

THE START OF THE WAR IN ASIA

When the superior Japanese forces conquered Manchuria in 1931, the Chinese had to accept that Japan controlled part of their country. On July 7, 1937 Chinese and Japanese forces clashed near Beijing in what became known as the "Marco Polo Bridge Incident". China and Japan were at war. They would continue fighting until the end of the Second World War in 1945. The Japanese swiftly conquered much of the north of China. The Japanese navy had successfully blockaded the whole of the Chinese coastline. By 1938 southern China was also in Japanese hands. The Japanese army came to a halt as it reached the mountains of central China. There was stalemate between the two countries although the Chinese fought a guerrilla campaign behind Japanese lines.

"I was standing in the Wilhelmplatz about noon when the loud speakers suddenly announced that England had declared itself at war with Germany. Some 250 people were standing in the sun. They listened attentively to the announcement. When it was finished there was not a murmur. They just stood as before. Stunned. The people cannot realise yet that Hitler has led them into a world war.

On the faces of the people astonishment, depression. Until today they have been going about their business pretty much as usual. There were food cards and soap cards and you couldn't get gasoline and at night it was difficult stumbling about in the dark. But the war in the west has seemed a bit far away to them."

William Shirer worked for the American CBS radio station. This was his report from Berlin on September 3, the day Germany found itself at war with France and Britain.

Above Hitler explores conquered Paris, in France. The iconic Eiffel Tower can be seen in the background.

"When all was clear and we were on the outskirts of Dunkirk we stopped on a long raised road with the canal on either side and nice big trees sheltering us from the air. We got out and looked up - there were about seventy bombers knocking hell out of the docks or what was left of them. From there to the beaches and they were black with troops waiting to go aboard only there were no boats. They gave us a raid this afternoon and evening and the following day they gave us a raid that lasted from dawn till dusk, about 17 hours. The fellows laid down on open beaches with the bombs falling alongside us, lucky it was sand, it killed the effect of the bombs."

Jack Toomey was a British soldier. He wrote this letter two weeks after he had been evacuated from Dunkirk.

The war in Europe began in the East as Germany invaded Poland. The conflict then turned westward as German troops swept all before them in the conquest of France and other countries including Norway and Belgium. Britain stood alone fighting against Germany, withstanding huge bombing raids on its major cities. The United States was reluctant to become directly involved in another large scale conflict, but all this changed when on December 7, 1941, Japanese planes attacked the US base of Pearl Harbour. The war had moved out of Europe and become a global conflict.

GERMAN EXPANSION

After the Germans had conquered Poland, Europe entered a period known as the "Phoney War". Although Britain and France were at war with Germany there was no fighting of any kind. But Hitler had ordered his generals to plan an attack on Western Europe. The "Phoney War" ended on April 9, 1940 when Germany attacked the Scandinavian countries Denmark and Norway so

that it could control the waters of the Atlantic. Denmark surrendered almost immediately. The British and the French came to the aid of the Norwegians. This slowed down the German advance, but the result was never in doubt, and Norway fell a few months later. The French and the British expected Germany to attack them next by sending troops to neighbouring Belgium. Instead, Germany decided to launch

Above The Northern European country of Norway held out against German attack until June 1940.

NORTH SEA

ENGLAND

UTRECHT

THE HAGUE

ROTTERDAM

BREDA

ANTWERP

NIEUPORT

DUNKIRK

CALAIS

BRUSSELS

GEMBLOUX

LILLE

BELGIUM

ENGLISH CHANNEL

ARRAS

ABBEVILLE

CAMBRAI

ST VALÉRY-EN-CAUX

CHERBOURG

SOMME

SEDAN

AISNE

SEINE

MEUSE

PARIS

FRANCE

JAN 8
Rationing begins in Britain.

APRIL 9
Nazis invade Denmark and Norway.

MAY 10
Nazis invade France, Belgium, Luxembourg and the Netherlands.

MAY 15
Holland surrenders to Nazis.

MAY 26
Evacuation of Allied troops from Dunkirk begins.

MAY 28
Belgium surrenders to Nazis.

Left Map showing the British and French evacuation of Dunkirk. The purple arrow represents Allied forces and the red arrows Axis troops.

its attack through an area south of Luxembourg called the Ardennes, which the French were defending only lightly.

TOWARDS DUNKIRK

The attack began on May 10, 1940. German tanks and soldiers smashed through the Ardennes, taking the French and British by surprise. On the same day German airborne troops landed in the Netherlands and Belgium. The Dutch army surrendered on May 14, hours after a heavy bombing raid on the city of Rotterdam, in the Netherlands. The German troops had advanced so quickly that by May 26, the British and French armies found themselves surrounded at a place called Dunkirk

"First shock – the streets are utterly deserted, the shops closed, the shutters down tight over all the windows. It was the emptiness that got you... Everyone lost his head. The government gave no lead. People were told to scoot, and at least three million of the five million in the city ran, ran without baggage, literally ran on their feet towards the south... The inhabitants are bitter at their government. It even forgot to tell the people until too late that Paris would not be defended.

Most of the German troops act like native tourists, and this proved a pleasant surprise to the Parisians. It seems funny, but every German soldier carries a camera. I saw them by the thousands today, photographing Notre-Dame, the Arc de Triomphe, the Invalides."

The American journalist William Shirer was a witness to the fall of Paris in June 1940.

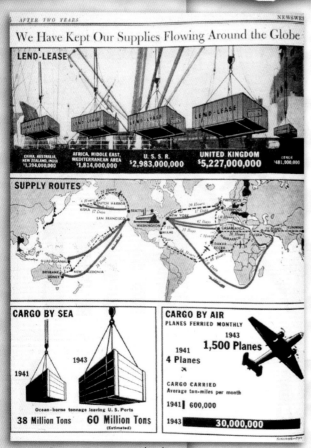

We Have Kept Our Supplies Flowing Around the Globe

LEND-LEASE

| CHINA, AUSTRALIA, NEW ZEALAND, INDIA $1,394,000,000 | AFRICA, MIDDLE EAST, MEDITERRANEAN AREA $1,814,000,000 | U.S.S.R. $2,983,000,000 | UNITED KINGDOM $5,227,000,000 | OTHER $481,000,000 |

SUPPLY ROUTES

CARGO BY SEA
Ocean-borne tonnage leaving U.S. Ports
1941 — 38 Million Tons
1943 — 60 Million Tons (Estimated)

CARGO BY AIR
PLANES FERRIED MONTHLY
1943 — 1,500 Planes
1941 — 4 Planes

CARGO CARRIED
Average ton-miles per month
1941 — 600,000
1943 — 30,000,000

Above Poster promoting US aid to the war effort – "Lend-Lease".

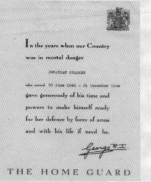

In the years when our Country was in mortal danger

JONATHAN STALKER

who served 20 June 1940 – 31 December 1944 gave generously of his time and powers to make himself ready for her defence by force of arms and with his life if need be.

George R.I.

THE HOME GUARD

Above A certificate of service in the Home Guard.

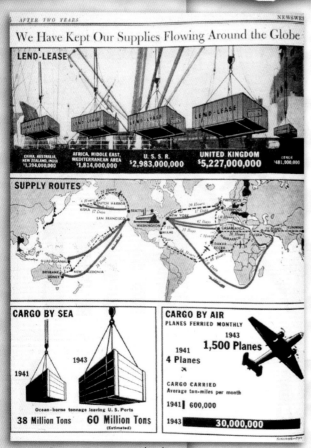

Above The British Spitfire (foreground) helped win the air battle against German planes such as the Messerschmitt Bf 109 (shown in the distance).

on the French coast. For the next two weeks British and French troops were evacuated from the Dunkirk beaches and shipped to England. The Belgians had surrendered on May 28. France was alone. The attack on France did not begin again until June 6. The French army could do little to stop the German advance. On June 17, the French leader Marshal Pétain offered to negotiate with the Germans. This negotiation was signed on June 22. Germany was given complete control of northern France and the Atlantic coast. Pétain then set up a new French government in Vichy in the south-east of France. The Vichy government ruled this part of France until the whole country was liberated in 1945.

BRITAIN ALONE

From June 1940 Hitler was in control of much of Europe. He had conquered Poland and successfully defeated Norway, Denmark, the Netherlands, Belgium and France. Now Britain was the only country that still faced the might of his armed forces. It looked hopeless. When the British retreated at Dunkirk, they had to leave behind nearly all their weapons and equipment. A few months earlier, Winston Churchill had replaced Neville Chamberlain as Prime Minister of Britain. Churchill was an inspirational war leader. His determination and rousing speeches made the British determined to fight on after so many defeats. Some people in the British

"Tonight, I am appealing to the heart and to the mind of every man and every woman within our borders who loves liberty. I ask you to consider the needs of our Nation and this hour, to put aside all personal differences until the victory is won. The light of democracy must be kept burning. To the perpetuation of this light, each of us must do his own share. The single effort of one individual may seem very small. But there are 130 million individuals over here. And there are many more millions in Britain and elsewhere bravely shielding the great flame of democracy from the blackout of barbarism. It is not enough for us merely to trim the wick, or polish the glass. The time has come when we must provide the fuel in ever-increasing amounts to keep that flame alight."

President Roosevelt talking to the American people about the Lend-Lease Act that he had just signed.

government wanted to negotiate with Hitler but Churchill believed that the British would never be defeated.

ATTACK FROM THE SKIES

With the fall of France, Hitler began to make plans for the invasion of Britain. That meant crossing the English Channel, and this could not be done until the Royal Air Force was destroyed. In July, 1940, the Battle of Britain began with German air attacks on ports and airfields. The Royal Air Force had an advantage over their German opponents. Radar let the British know in advance whenever a German attack was coming in and

Left *In 1940, Winston Churchill became Prime Minister of Great Britain. His radio speeches strengthened the nation's determination to win the war.*

"Paid visit to town and was on my way home by train when a flight of planes roared overhead. There came a series of explosions followed by a continuous rattle like pebbles falling on galvanised steel sheeting. The train pulled into a suburban station, the porters shouting 'Air Raid - Take Cover'. This was the real thing. Passengers poured calmly out of the subway... Going out on to the platform I joined a small group gazing into the sky... The sky was blue and almost cloudless. There were puffs of bursting shells, the rattle of machine guns and the tiny shapes of our own interceptor planes darting into the swarm."

The diary entry of an unknown Londoner describing a fight during the Battle of Britain.

TIMELINE 1940

JUNE 4
Dunkirk evacuation ends.

JUNE 10
Italy declares war on Britain and France

JUNE 14
German forces enter Paris.

JUNE 22
France signs armistice with the Nazis.

JULY 5
Vichy government breaks off relations with Britain.

JULY 10
Battle of Britain begins.

Below *During the bombing of Britain, children were evacuated from the cities to the relative safety of the countryside.*

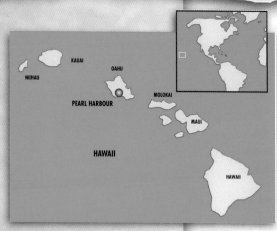

Above *The US base of Pearl Harbour is situated in the Hawaiian Islands in the central Pacific Ocean. The islands became a US territory in 1900.*

Below *After the attack on Pearl Harbour, President Franklin D. Roosevelt took the United States into World War II.*

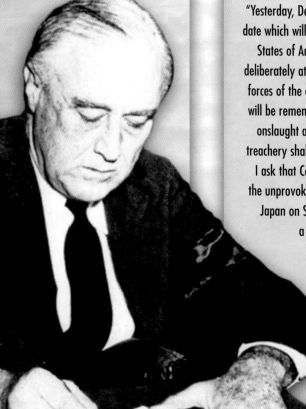

they were able to send their own planes to meet them. By September 1940 Hitler realised that he could not defeat the British in the air. Invasion plans were postponed. Hitler tried to defeat the British people by ordering bombing raids on their towns and cities. These raids were called the Blitz, short for "blitzkrieg" or "lightning war". The Blitz began in September 7, 1940 when London was bombed and more than 400 people died. London was attacked many times until the bombing ended in May 1941. Other cities such as Glasgow, Coventry and Portsmouth were also heavily bombed.

"Yesterday, December seventh, 1941 – a date which will live in infamy – the United States of America was suddenly and deliberately attacked by the naval and air forces of the empire of Japan… Always will be remembered the character of the onslaught against us… this form of treachery shall never endanger us again. I ask that Congress declare that since the unprovoked and dastardly attack by Japan on Sunday, December seventh, a state of war has existed between the United States and the Japanese empire."

President Roosevelt speaking to the American people the day after the attack on Pearl Harbour.

TOWARDS A WORLD WAR

Throughout the early years of the Second World War the American government remained neutral. This was known as "isolationism". After the First World War many Americans did not want to involve the United States in fighting between other countries. Despite this, the British were helped in their resistance against Germany by the American President, Franklin D. Roosevelt. The United States was still officially a neutral country, but there was a lot of public support for the British. In March 1941, the American Congress passed the Lend–Lease Act. It allowed Britain to buy or rent weapons and other military equipment from the United States. Americans were very worried about the expansion of Japanese influence. The United States government did not allow the Japanese to buy steel, iron or fuel for planes from them. From July 25, 1941 the Americans also prevented Japanese access to any money that they held abroad. This meant that the Japanese could not buy any metals or fuel, which would bring the Japanese armed forces to a standstill.

Above *The Blitz decimated parts of London, including this section of the East End.*

Above *A monument to the USS Oklahoma on the grounds of the United States Capitol.*

TIMELINE
1940-1941

SEPT 7, 1940
The German Blitz against England begins.

SEPT 16, 1940
United States military conscription bill passed.

NOV 5, 1940
Roosevelt re-elected as U.S president.

MARCH 11, 1941
President Roosevelt signs the Lend-Lease Act.

JULY 26, 1941
Roosevelt freezes Japanese assets in United States.

AUG 20, 1941
Nazi siege of Leningrad begins.

DEC 7, 1941
Japan bombs Pearl Harbour.

DEC 8, 1941
United States and Britain declare war on Japan.

HORROR IN HAWAII

Because of these strict sanctions, Japan began to formulate a plan. It decided to attack the American Pacific Fleet at Pearl Harbour, on the island of Hawaii in the Pacific. This was because Japan believed that these ships would be used against them if it tried to control more of Asia. Early on the morning of December 7, 1941, Japanese aircraft attacked the fleet at Pearl Harbour. In the unexpected attack, 2,403 Americans were killed, including 68 civilians. Many more were wounded. In under two hours the Japanese had destroyed or damaged eight battleships, three cruisers and 30 destroyers. The Japanese lost less than thirty aircraft but the Americans lost four hundred. On December 8, President Roosevelt spoke to the American people and declared war on Japan. Three days later, on December 11, 1941, Italy and Germany declared war on the United States. The war was now being fought around the world.

Above *The Japanese attack on Pearl Harbour took just one hour and 15 minutes.*

"Men were screaming and trying to get aboard our ship and get out of the water. When I got to my gun, there were a few of the others there. We threw the gun cover over the side of the gun tube. And stood there cussing and crying at the Japs! You would be scared for a while and then you would get mad and cuss. After a while we finally got ammo up to our gun. But we had to put it into clips before it could be fired. I don't know how long a time this was. But the 'Oklahoma' had rolled over on her side. And the harbour was pretty well afire by this time. The smoke and the fire was all around us.

Then somebody yelled planes overhead. We trained the gun around and started firing. One of the planes fell up in front of us on Ford Island. I don't know who hit it, but it was one down."

Seaman Harlan Eisnaugle describes the Japanese attack on Pearl Harbour.

November 20, 1941

"I slept a few hours on something that goes by the name of bed. The houses all look as if they had witnessed some fierce fighting and that the Germans got the worst of it. Helmets, machine-gun equipment, blood-stained clothes and the like were scattered anyhow in the straw.

November 29

Already in the summer the thought had occurred to me once that really this country was made for winter, for snow and icy cold... Oh Russia, what have you still in store for us, what cruelties will you still inflict upon us?"

Diary entries of German army Field Pastor Sebacher

When the Germans were confident that they were secure in the west of Europe, they turned their attention towards the richest prize of all – the Soviet Union. The German attack on the Soviet Union seemed unstoppable. In the end, it was only halted at the gates of Moscow.

STALIN AND HITLER

Nazi Germany and the Soviet Union had signed a non-aggression pact in August, 1939. Stalin knew that Hitler wanted to invade the Soviet Union and he thought that this pact would give him time to build up his forces. Hitler signed the pact to make sure that he could invade Poland without the Soviet Union getting in his way. But Hitler never had any intention of keeping his word. The pact was just a useful tool, which he thought would keep the Soviet Union quiet while he dealt with Poland and conquered Western Europe. When that had been done, he began to plan his attack on the Soviet Union.

SPACE TO GROW

Hitler believed that the German people needed what was called "Lebensraum" or "living space". This meant that the German Empire had to expand eastwards into Poland and the Soviet Union. Hitler saw the people who already lived there as inferior to the Germans, believing that they should be driven out. The attack on the Soviet Union began on June 22, 1941, and was known as "Operation Barbarossa". In the months before, Stalin had refused to send troops closer to the border with Germany in case that annoyed Hitler. Now the Soviet army found itself unprepared for what became the largest attack in the history of the Second World War. Just over three million troops crossed the Soviet border on that day and they met little resistance.

Right Soviet soldiers were used to fighting in icy conditions, a factor which helped them to repel Hitler's army.

Above *The Soviet army turned every building into a fortress as they fought to defeat the Germans at Stalingrad.*

TIMELINE
1941-1942

DEC 11, 1941
Germany declares war on the United States.

JAN 1, 1942
Declaration of the United Nations signed by 26 Allied nations.

JAN 20, 1942
Wannsee Conference held by Nazis to discuss the "Final Solution of the Jewish Question".

VICTORY IN RUSSIA

The tactic of "blitzkrieg" (lightning war), which had worked so well in Poland and Western Europe, was again used in this attack. The German army swept into the Soviet Union, covering vast distances in only a few weeks, and capturing more than one million Soviet troops. Hitler was determined to take the cities of Leningrad and Moscow before the end of the year. He ordered his troops to push forward. By September, the German army was less than 20 miles from Moscow and just outside Leningrad. But here they came to a halt. The freezing winter had begun to set in, and the Germans were not ready for it.

Above *An anti-Soviet poster issued by the Nazi party.*

Right *German troops reached the outskirts of Moscow. Here they parade prisoners in the streets.*

"After the news I ran out to the street. Panic was spreading across the city. People hastily exchanged a few words, then rushed to the shops, buying anything they saw. They were running in the streets like mad. Many went to the savings bank to take out their deposits. This wave absorbed me too. I also tried to receive cash from my savings bank. But I came too late. The bank was empty, payments had been stopped... Only in the evening everything became strangely quiet. It seemed that everybody had hidden somewhere, possessed by terror."

Elena Skriyabina writes in her diary about the way that the people of Leningrad reacted to the news of the German invasion.

Above *The British battleship HMS Repulse helped chase the German Bismarck, and was sunk by Japanese bombers near Malaya.*

of a grand Japanese plan to dominate the Pacific and large areas of Asia. The Japanese attack was quick and relentless, but just like the Germans, the Japanese were eventually slowed down and finally stopped. When the Japanese offensive began, both Britain and America controlled parts of Asia and the Pacific, and moved to protect them. Their actions were too little and too late. Only weeks after Pearl Harbour the Japanese took the Pacific islands of Guam and Wake Island from the Americans. On Christmas Day, British-held Hong Kong fell to Japan. In February 1942, a small Japanese army defeated a far larger British force in Singapore, in what was seen as one of the greatest failures in the history of the British army. In March 1942, Japanese forces had invaded Bursa and tens of

Soviet resistance was also far stronger than Hitler had anticipated. German troops besieged Leningrad for 900 days, but did not succeed in taking it. Moscow, too, held out. The Soviet Union had begun the task of pushing the German army back.

JAPAN ADVANCES

The attack on Pearl Harbour on December 7, 1941 was only the start

"The tank was hit and the plane caught fire so I jumped. I had to parachute from dangerously low down, but I survived. The parachute opened with a bang and I hurtled to sea. When I looked around, I saw three pillars of smoke far away. I later learned that our three aircraft carriers, Akagi, Kaga and Soryu, had been destroyed… I thought it was all over. We had no carriers to counter attack. There was nothing we could do."

Pilot Iyozo Fujita fought at both Pearl Harbour and the Battle of Midway. This extract was written after the Battle of Midway.

"The weird noise is the first thing that I remember about the jungle… The birds sounded like dogs barking… and the men were jittery initially when they first got there, they were shooting at everything that moved, but I finally convinced my squad that we didn't have much ammunition, that they couldn't waste any."

An American soldier named Kerry Lane recalls arriving on a Pacific island to fight the Japanese.

thousands of refugees fled north to the border with India. Dutch-held Java surrendered, under air and land attack, and 100,000 Dutch, British, US and Australian troops were taken prisoner. The attack on the American-held Philippines began on December 8, 1941, with bombing raids. Two weeks later the land attack by Japan began. The American troops fought well but surrendered on the Bataan peninsula on April 9, 1942. On May 6, US and Filipino troops surrendered on Corregidor Island.

FIGHTING AT SEA

Japanese military leaders were so confident that they decided to conquer even more lands. They focused on Port Moresby in New Guinea. American ships sailed in a bid to stop the Japanese invasion fleet, and the Battle of the Coral Sea was fought on May 7 and 8, 1942. Only planes from aircraft carriers were used, so US and Japanese ships never saw each other. This time, Japan was forced back. The Japanese also tried to conquer Midway, an island close to Hawaii. In the first week of June, the Japanese navy set sail. The losses of Pearl Harbour meant the Americans had only a small fleet left to defend Midway. But they broke

Above *A Japanese reconstruction of the British surrender at Singapore.*

Japanese codes and found out what they were planning. On June 4, 1942, US planes destroyed three Japanese aircraft carriers in just one five-minute strike, and a fourth one at the end of the day. Midway was a massive defeat, and the Japanese never recovered.

TIMELINE 1942

FEB, 1942
British forces defeated by Japanese at Singapore.

MAY 4-8
Allies win Battle of Coral Sea.

MAY 30
First British air raid on Cologne, Germany. where a thousand bombs were dropped.

JUNE 4
US wins Battle of Midway.

Below *Japanese troops celebrate victory in Hong Kong in 1941.*

Left *A US Marine pin. US marines defeated the Japanese in the Battle of Midway.*

> "The Japanese army fed off the Philippines. They didn't bring any supplies; they ate up what we had grown for us to eat, so there was a lot of hunger and despair... They were very cruel, even to passers-by in the street. They would slap you down if you didn't greet them, if you didn't bow profusely enough, and there was a lot of hardship."
>
> *Carmen Guerra Nakpil remembers how the Japanese behaved once they had conquered the Philippines.*

✉ LETTER 📰 NEWSPAPER ARTICLE 🎙 OFFICIAL SPEECH ⬭ PLAQUE/INSCRIPTION 📠 TELEGRAM   **23**

WORLD WAR II

"The hospitals were crammed. All preparations counted for nothing. You could travel without a ticket on the train, bicycle on the pavements. There were no windows in the trains, no schools, no doctors, no post, no telephone. One felt completely cut off from the world. To meet a friend who survived was a wonderful experience. There was no water, no light, no fire. A candle was of priceless value. Little children collected wood from the ruins for cooking. Every family dug its own toilet in the garden."

Klaus Schmidt describing what the German city of Darmstadt was like after a British air raid in 1944.

Above *German Dornier 217 aircraft on the offensive over the Silvertown area of London's Dockland in the autumn of 1940.*

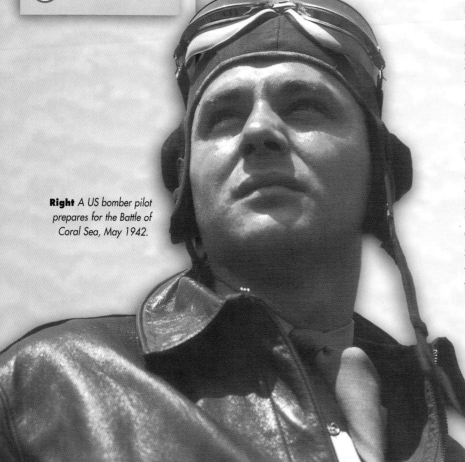

Right *A US bomber pilot prepares for the Battle of Coral Sea, May 1942.*

WAR IN THE AIR

The Second World War was fought in a way that was completely different from any other conflict in history. For the first time, fighting in the air played a central part in the results of many battles. The Battles of Britain, Coral Sea and Midway were all fought by aircraft. In the Pacific, aircraft did not fight each other but were used to attack ships. Both the Americans and the British believed heavy bombing of German and Japanese military and civilian targets would shorten the war. The Americans were able to produce huge numbers of aircraft for the war effort. Between 1940 and 1945, factories in America built more than 300, 000 war planes. Many of these were large bombers, like the B-17 and the B-29.

CITY ATTACK

The bombing of civilian targets was known as "area bombing". Although the Germans and Japanese did bomb towns and cities it was mainly the British

Above *A reconstructed B-17 bomber, currently residing in Sweden, Europe.*

Below *B-17 planes launch a wave of attacks over Berlin during 1942.*

and the Americans who waged this kind of warfare. In the last years of the war more than 100 German cities were bombed, nearly four million houses destroyed and almost a million civilians died. Cities such as Hamburg and Dresden were almost completely destroyed. When American bombers could reach the mainland, heavy bombing of Japan's cities began. The Japanese suffered even more than the Germans, because their houses were often wooden and very close together. This meant that fires started by bombs could spread quickly. On March 10, 1945, American planes took part in one of the heaviest raids of the war. More than 250,000 buildings were destroyed and nearly 100,000 people died. Some bombing raids were so heavy they caused fire storms. The heat from fires makes air rise, to be replaced by cool air. This fans the flames and makes the fire hotter, so the air rises even faster, creating a wind so strong that the flames burn everything. Many people died in these fire storms.

TIMELINE 1942-43

JULY 5, 1942
Soviet resistance in the Crimea ends.

JULY 9, 1942
Germans begin a drive towards Stalingrad

AUG 23, 1942
German air raid on Stalingrad.

SEPT 13, 1942
Battle of Stalingrad begins.

NOV 19, 1942
Soviets counter-attack at Stalingrad.

FEB 2, 1943
German troops at Stalingrad surrender after 3 months of extremely intense fighting.

SEPT 3, 1943
Allies land on Italian mainland. Italy signs secret armistice with Allies.

NOV 28, 1943
"Big Three" of Roosevelt, Stalin and Churchill meet at Tehran.

"Suddenly there was a roar like an express train, a hurtling, a tearing, all-powerful overwhelming rush. Together we sprang to our feet. We got no further. The earth seemed to split into a thousand fragments… Outside there was a stifling, forbidding atmosphere. I stumbled over two masses of debris, clattered over piles of glass. The moon shone wanly upon this uncanny nightmare. Women in the hall were dizzy. I rushed outside in the front. I saw at once all the windows of the flats had been blasted open or out."

Colin Perry describes what happened when an explosion hit his parents' house during a German bombing raid in London on October 18, 1940.

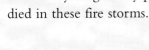

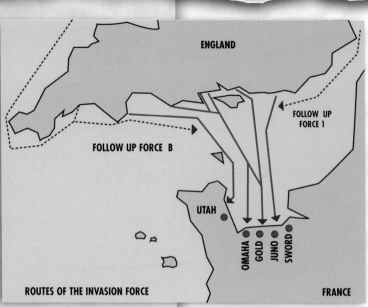

ROUTES OF THE INVASION FORCE

ENGLAND

FOLLOW UP FORCE 1

FOLLOW UP FORCE B

UTAH

OMAHA GOLD JUNO SWORD

FRANCE

Above Map showing the D-Day invasion routes.

The end of the Second World War was several years coming. The German army was slowly pushed backwards by Allied troops in Eastern Europe, France and Italy. The D-Day landing was one of the largest military operations ever to have taken place. In Asia and the Pacific the Japanese fought to the death rather than suffer the dishonour of surrender. In the end a devastating new bomb used on two cities in Japan brought the Second World War to an end.

"We go to the centre of Stalingrad to bring some logs for the construction of the bunker. The impression from Stalingrad is terrible. A few stone buildings which had been there were razed to the ground during the air raid. Wooden buildings had been dismantled by the infantry to build bunkers, so that Stalingrad is completely in ruins. One can say that Stalingrad does not exist any more. It is 15 degrees below zero."

A diary entry from a German soldier called Heinz W. He was taken prisoner by the Soviet army.

BATTLE OF STALINGRAD

The German advance into the Soviet Union had been halted outside Moscow. Neither the Soviet nor the German armies could defeat each other. In August 1942 Hitler ordered Stalingrad to be taken and diverted a huge army to attack it. The Germans advanced into Stalingrad and were soon involved in fighting street by street. In November Soviet forces encircled the city, trapping more than 200,000 German troops, then attacked. Hitler ordered German troops never to surrender, but on February 1, 1943, when the remnants of the German army caved in, Stalingrad was the beginning of the end for the Nazis.

D-DAY INVASION

To help the Soviet troops, British and American forces planned an invasion of occupied Europe. The German army was pushed out of North Africa, then in July its ally, Italy, was invaded. The British and the Americans knew they had to liberate Western Europe by landing on the French coast. On June 6, 1944, British and American troops landed on the beaches of

Left A building in Stalingrad burns during the German onslaught of August 1942.

Normandy on what was called D-Day. It was the largest sea-borne invasion in history. A vast armada of 2,727 steamers and merchant ships and 700 warships made for the landing grounds. The first few hundred infantrymen were sent in, followed by parachute troops. By the following morning 18,000 British and American troops had landed by parachute, and the first wave of American ground troops landed in an area code-named Utah Beach. British, American and Canadian troops followed thick and fast. German resistance was strong, but they were pushed back. On July 25, 1944, American troops broke out of Normandy and advanced rapidly. On August 25,

Above *Crowds take to the streets on V-E Day, celebrating Germany's surrender in World War II.*

Left *The Purple Heart medal is awarded to US personnel wounded or killed during active service.*

French and American forces liberated Paris. British troops pushed north from Normandy to liberate the Netherlands and Belgium. On December 16, a strong German force broke the US-held front in the Belgian Ardennes, penetrating into Belgium and causing a "bulge" in Allied lines.

TIMELINE 1944

JAN 6, 1944
Soviet Army advances into Poland.

JAN 27
Red Army breaks 900-day siege of Leningrad.

JAN 31
American forces invade Kwajalein.

JUNE 6
D-Day.

JUNE 15
American marines invade Saipan.

AUG 25
Paris liberated.

OCT 23-26
U.S. naval forces destroy remnants of Japanese Navy at the Battle of Leyte Gulf.

"This is D-Day', came the announcement over the British radio and quite rightly, 'This is the day.' The invasion has begun!

Great commotion on the Secret Annexe! Would the long-awaited liberation that has been talked of so much, but which still seems too wonderful, too much like a fairy tale, ever come true? We don't know yet, but hope is revived within us, it gives us fresh courage, and makes us strong again.
... the best part of the invasion is that I have the feeling that our friends are approaching. We have been oppressed by those terrible Germans for so long, they have had their knives at our throats, that the thought of friends and delivery fills us with confidence."

An extract from the diary of Anne Frank. Anne was a Jewish girl who hid with her family in Amsterdam from the Nazi occupiers.

Above *A soldier raises the Soviet flag over the Reichstag during the fall of Germany and the Third Reich, May 1945.*

"Some Japs crawled up out of their holes in the early hours of the morning and charged our foxholes. They crawled to within 10 feet of one fellow and started yelling, 'Hey, Corpsman.' Our fellow asked him for the password, but he still yelled, 'Hey, Corpsman.' All he wanted was for some fellow to show himself so the Jap could throw a hand grenade in his hole. The kid saw him and killed him. When they pull one of their banzai charges, they gather together in a big group and start yelling. Then some of their officers start waving swords above their heads and shout, 'Banzai, banzai!' While they scream, they charge. Of course our guns cut them down like flies, Milly, but it is scary listening to them scream like that."

An American soldier, Tom Kennedy, writes a letter to his wife about the fighting on Iwo Jima.

Right *In a desperate effort to revive their fortunes, the Japanese revived the name Kamikaze and applied it to the suicide missions of their air force, where planes deliberately crashed into Allied ships.*

US forces, under the temporary command of Field Marshal Montgomery, bravely held out until they were relieved by Allied troops. By January 14, 1945, German forces had been routed. In the first few months of 1945, British, American and Soviet troops crossed into Germany in a race to see who could reach Berlin first. In the end it was the Soviet troops. On April 16, 1945, the Soviet Union began its attack on Berlin. Eight days later the city was encircled. On April 30, Hitler killed himself as Soviet shells exploded around him. A week later Germany surrendered. The war in Europe was over, but the war in the Pacific went on.

JAPAN ON DEFENSIVE

After the Battle of Midway, Japan was on the defensive. Although the US was losing as many ships and planes as Japan it could replace them far faster. The Japanese had to defend a large amount of territory but with fewer and fewer weapons. In the summer of 1942 they occupied the island of Guadalcanal as part of their assault on Port Moresby. The US attacked Guadalcanal on August 7, 1942, but it was not until February 1943 that the Japanese were finally cleared out. From May 1943, the Americans began "island-hopping", attacking some of the Japanese-held Pacific islands and ignoring others. The aim was to capture an island with an airfield

Above *The Japanese officially surrendered on the USS Missouri on Sept 2, 1945.*

TIMELINE 1945

FEB 4-11, 1945
Roosevelt, Churchill and Stalin meet at Yalta Conference

APRIL 12
President Roosevelt dies and Truman becomes President.

APRIL 30
Adolf Hitler commits suicide.

MAY 8
Victory in Europe (VE) Day.

AUG 6-9
Atomic bombs dropped on Hiroshima and Nagasaki

AUG 15
Victory over Japan (VJ) Day.

and start to bomb the Japanese mainland. They achieved this on August 10, 1944 when Saipan and Guam were taken.

ENDGAME

The first major battle of 1945 began when US forces tried to take back Manila, the capital of the Philippines. Japan fought on until the war ended. In February, 1945, US troops landed on the island of Iwo Jima, which they needed as a base from which to protect bombers flying over Japan. The battle for Iwo Jima lasted for just under a month and cost the lives of more than six thousand Americans and more than 20,000 Japanese. In June, 1945, the US lost 12,000 soldiers during the capture of the island of Okinawa, and 110,000 Japanese died. The US knew many thousands of people would die in an invasion of the Japanese mainland. This was one reason why, at the start of August, President Truman allowed atomic bombs to be dropped on Hiroshima and Nagasaki. These bombs killed about 120,000 people and Japan surrendered on August 14. The war in the Pacific, and the rest of the world, was over.

Above *The horrific damage wrought by the atomic bomb dropped on Hiroshima in August 1945.*

"I can never forget the sight of those people. They were burnt so badly that they didn't look human. Half of their ears were gone and their eyes were crushed. They didn't look like human beings. A person next to me said in a strained voice, 'Help me! Give me water!' The next moment he was dead. Many people lost their hair, bled from their gums, got a rash on their bodies."

Suzuko Numata remembers what happened to her when the atomic bomb fell on Hiroshima.

You never know who's on the wires!

BE CAREFUL WHAT YOU SAY

Above *A British propaganda poster reminded the public to beware of possible German spies in their midst.*

The Second World War affected people in a way that had not happened before. Newsreel films showed what was happening almost immediately, and governments used propaganda, or positive publicity, to keep people on their side. Everyone – military and civilian, young and old, male or female – seemed to be involved in the war effort. In times of war the arts, including music, painting, poetry, theatre and cinema usually flourish, and this was very true in World War II. It allowed people the chance to escape, at least for a while, from the worries and dangers of war.

1 In all reports Warsaw is not to be described as a town but as a fortress.

2 Where possible, shoot film on a larger scale than previously of Jewish types of all kinds from Warsaw… not only whilst working but also character studies. This material should lead to a strengthening of anti-Semitic instruction in our domestic policies and in foreign affairs.

Propaganda Instructions of the Reichs Propaganda Ministry for October 2, 1939. German film-makers and radio broadcasters were given clear instructions in how to report the war.

Right *Joseph Goebbels (far right) was responsible for Nazi propaganda.*

PROPAGANDA

During the Second World War all governments tried to make sure their own people supported the war effort. Propaganda is a kind of advertising in which people are encouraged to believe certain things. It can be done in many ways, including film, leaflets, books, newspapers or radio broadcasts. Governments also used propaganda to try to weaken the enemy. For instance,

both the Germans and British dropped leaflets from planes on each other's cities, trying to convince people that they were on the losing side. One of the best-known forms of propaganda of the Second World War was the poster. These were quick and easy to produce, and very colourful and eye-catching. Different countries used different messages on their posters. The Germans warned of the menace of Soviet communism. The Soviet Union appealed to the patriotism of its many different peoples. The British used images of the countryside to show people what they were fighting for.

Above Nazi poster depicting a demonic American soldier captured by a serene looking Adolf Hitler.

THE ROLE OF BROADCASTING

Very few people had television in the Second World War but most people had a radio. This meant that each country could broadcast propaganda to the enemy as well as to their own people. Germany's most famous broadcaster was William Joyce, known as "Lord Haw-Haw". His broadcasts were meant to make the people of Britain less willing to fight. An American-born Japanese woman, "Tokyo Rose", broadcast radio messages designed to discourage American troops. The British Broadcasting Corporation (BBC) broadcast all over occupied Europe, and encouraged people to draw the letter V (for victory) in Morse code, or dot dot dot dash. Chalked Morse code "V"s appeared everywhere as an act of defiance against the German conquerors.

Right William Joyce, known as Lord Haw Haw, was Goebbels' anti-British mouthpiece. He was captured at the Danish border near Flensburg, and later tried and executed.

TIMELINE
1946-49

MAR, 1946
Churchill gives Iron Curtain speech.

MAR, 1947
Announcement of Truman Doctrine.

JUNE, 1947
Marshall Plan announced in US.

MAY, 1948
Israel created.

AUG, 1949
USSR tests Atomic bomb.

OCT, 1949
East Germany created.

"The terrific casualties suffered by Allied forces in the first ten days of the invasion, which show that the British government has not the slightest regard for the life of its soldiers, have been compared by the highest German military experts with the useless slaughter of British troops... in the last war. British troops have been forced into tank traps when storming bridges, in such numbers that literally mountains of dead bodies have to be climbed over by those following behind. There is no need for me to give details of this terrible and useless massacre because those of you who are now taking part in the fighting are fully aware of what is going on."

German propaganda broadcast to British troops in France soon after D-Day.

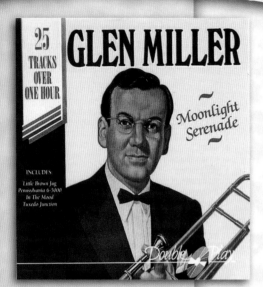

Above *Moonlight Serenade was one of many musical numbers made popular by the Glen Miller Orchestra.*

THE WAR IN FILM

Thousands of films were made during the war. Few involved battle or fighting scenes, though many "war" films were made later. Musicals, comedies and detective stories were very popular. The best-known film of the war years, *Casablanca*, told of Rick and Ilsa, played by Humphrey Bogart and Ingrid Bergman, who had to leave each other to fight the Germans, something millions were also having to do.

THE WAR IN MUSIC

During the war, people turned to music that helped them to forget their troubles for a while. Berlin-born actress and singer Marlene Dietrich was popular with both German and British troops. Vera Lynn broadcast songs in Britain and sang for troops in Europe and Asia. One of the most popular musicians was American Glen Miller. His big band tunes, were played in dance halls in America and Britain. His small plane vanished over the English Channel in 1944 but it is not known exactly how he died.

Oh! I have slipped the surly bonds of earth

And danced the skies on laughter-silvered wings;

Sunward I've climbed and joined the tumbling mirth

Of sun-split clouds, and done a hundred things

You have not dreamed of: wheeled and soared and swung

High in the sunlit silence. Hov'ring there,

I've chased the shouting wind along, and flung

My eager craft through footless falls of air...

Up, up the long, delirious, burning blue

I've topped the wind-swept heights with easy grace

Where never lark, nor even eagle flew -

And, while with silent lifting mind I've trod

The high, untrespassed sanctity of space,

Put out my hand and touched the face of God.

 High Flight *by John Magee*

Right *Released in 1942, Casablanca is set in occupied Africa during the early days of World War II.*

BOOKS AND THE WAR

Reading was a popular pastime during the war, especially crime fiction. British novelist Dorothy L. Sayers' hero was the upper-class detective Lord Peter Whimsey. American Ed McBain's 87th precinct detective novels were eagerly awaited. During the war, a young Jewish girl wrote about her experiences hiding from the Nazis in Amsterdam. She was betrayed, taken to Belsen concentration camp, and died in 1945. Her father survived and published *The Diary of Anne Frank* in 1947. The suffering and sacrifices made by people everywhere inspired many poets. One of the most famous was Canadian John Magee, who was a Pilot Officer in the R.A.F. His poem *High Flight* describes how he felt as he flew. The poem was used by President Ronald Reagan in 1986, in a service to mark the lives of the astronauts who died on the space shuttle *Challenger*. John Magee was killed in a mid-air collision on December 11, 1941. He was 19. After the war, many people wrote about their wartime experiences, including Italian Jew Primo Levi, who was one of few people to survive the Auschwitz camp.

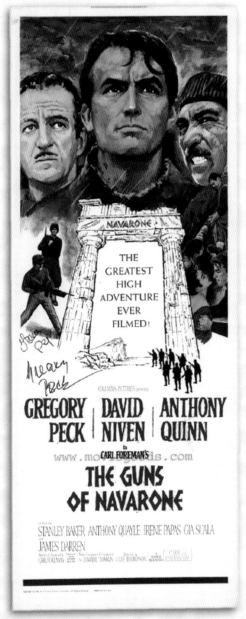

Above War films were popular long after 1945. The Guns of Navarone (1961) tells of a British team sent to destroy a gun emplacement in occupied Greek territory.

TIMELINE
1949-1954

1949
People's Republic of China proclaimed by Mao Tse-tung. NATO – a military alliance between America and western European states – formed.

1950
Korean war starts.

1954
Vietnam declares independence from France.

Below Vera Lynn was one of Britain's premier entertainers during the war and kept up the spirits of the public when times were difficult.

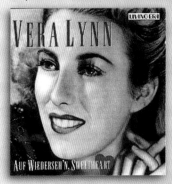

RICK: You have any idea what you'd have to look forward to if you stayed here? Nine chances out of ten, we'd both wind up in a concentration camp...

ILSA: You're saying this only to make me go.

RICK: I'm saying it because it's true. Inside, we both know you belong with Victor...if that plane leaves the ground and you're not with him, you'll regret it...

ILSA: But what about us?

RICK: We'll always have Paris. We didn't have, we , we lost it until you came to Casablanca. We got it back last night.

ILSA: When I said I would never leave you.

RICK: And you never will. But I've got a job to do too. What I've got to do, you can't be any part of, Ilsa...

Part of the script of Casablanca.

Above *In the aftermath of victory, the Soviet Union, led by Joseph Stalin, found itself engaged in a new kind of struggle with the United States – the Cold War.*

As the Second World War drew to a close, the seeds of a new kind of conflict were sown. Those who had fought together separated into two different camps dominated by the United States and the Soviet Union. They did not fight each other directly, and so this period was known as the Cold War. In the 21st century a new kind of conflict began with the attack on the World Trade Center in New York.

A NEW KIND OF WAR

Since 1941 the United States, Britain and the Soviet Union had fought together against common enemies. After the defeat of Germany and Japan in 1945 the alliance began to come apart. America and the Soviet Union began to look at each other with suspicion. Stalin wanted to make sure Germany could not be a threat to him again.

He made sure the countries bordering the Soviet Union had communist governments that he could control. The Americans and the British wanted to stop the spread of communism and create democracies. Europe was divided into a pro-American West and a pro-Soviet East.

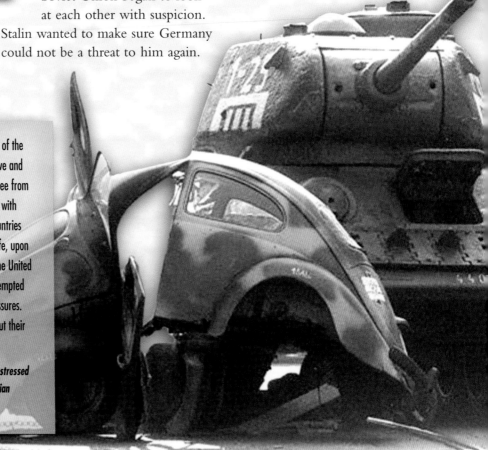

"One of the primary objectives of the foreign policy of the United States is the creation of conditions in which we and other nations will be able to work out a way of life free from coercion. This was a fundamental issue in the war with Germany and Japan. Our victory was won over countries which sought to impose their will, and their way of life, upon other nations. I believe that it must be the policy of the United States to support free peoples who are resisting attempted subjugation by armed minorities or by outside pressures. I believe that we must assist free peoples to work out their own destinies in their own way."

In this famous address to Congress, President Truman stressed the duty of the United States to combat totalitarian regimes worldwide. March 12, 1947.

Above *The Berlin Wall was erected in August 1961, and was one of the most potent symbols of the Cold War.*

1955
Warsaw Pact created, aligning several Eastern European states with the Soviet Union.

1961
Work on Berlin Wall begins. US troops arrive in Vietnam.

1962
Cuban Missile Crisis.

1967
Six Day War in Middle East ends with Israel gaining substantial territory.

1973
Yom Kippur war. Cease-fire agreement signed in Vietnam but fighting continues.

1975
Vietnam war ends. Vietnam reunited the following year.

The mistrust between these two groups was known as the Cold War.

TAKING SIDES

In Europe the Cold War was most clearly seen in the defeated Germany. In 1945 Germany was divided between its occupying powers. Berlin was also divided, even though it was in the middle of Soviet-occupied Germany. In 1948 the Soviets blocked access to Berlin by road and rail to try to drive out Britain, France and the United States. They responded with a massive air lift which supplied their forces and fed the two million people of Berlin. The Berlin Air Lift continued for 15 months and made the world aware of what was happening.

In 1949, the Americans and the British helped to form the North Atlantic Treaty Organisation, a military alliance opposed to the Soviet Union, which responded with its own military alliance, the Warsaw Pact. The Soviet Union wanted East Germany, which it controlled, to be a separate country. Many people tried to escape to West Germany. In August 1961 the Soviets built a wall through Berlin to stop them escaping. Troops from NATO and the Warsaw Pact faced each other across a divided Germany.

Left *After the Nazis were defeated, the Soviets took over much of Eastern Europe, including Czechoslovakia. This photograph is a reconstruction of the Russian entry into Prague.*

"A lady saw my Berlin Airlift Veterans Association shirt. She stopped me and said, 'You are the first person I have ever met who participated in the Berlin Airlift and I would like to thank you for giving me life.' We had a little talk and she explained to me that she was a four-year-old when the blockade started. She got her first taste of chocolate from a candy bar dropped by the 'Candy Bomber'. We, the members of BAVA, firmly believe that the Berlin Airlift put the first big chink in the defeat of communism."

William Gross is the current Secretary / Treasurer of the Berlin Airlift Veterans association.

"While the wall is the most obvious and vivid demonstration of the failures of the Communist system – for all the world to see – we take no satisfaction in it; for it is, as your Mayor has said, an offense not only against history but an offense against humanity, separating families, dividing husbands and wives and brothers and sisters, and dividing a people who wish to be joined together.

What is true of this city is true of Germany: real, lasting peace in Europe can never be assured as long as one German out of four is denied the elementary right of free men, and that is to make a free choice. In 18 years of peace and good faith, this generation of Germans has earned the right to be free, including the right to unite their families and their nation in lasting peace, with good will to all people."

President John F Kennedy speaking at the Berlin Wall on June 26, 1963. It was one of his most famous speeches.

Above *Jewish refugees begin to arrive in Israel after the creation of the state in 1948.*

THE COLD WAR IN ASIA

Between 1950 and 1953 communist North Korea and American-backed South Korea fought in the Korean War. The Soviet Union and the United States also backed different sides in the Vietnam War, which lasted from 1961 to 1975 and ended in defeat for America. 50,000 American soldiers died in Vietnam.

BIRTH OF A STATE

After the end of World War II, many world governments supported the creation of the state of Israel. Six million Jewish people had been killed by the Nazis during

Below *A United States soldier tends to a wounded comrade during the Vietnam war.*

the war, in what is known as the Holocaust. Many people agreed that there should be a Jewish homeland. Land was allocated from the state of Palestine in the Middle East. Palestine had been controlled by the British since 1919, and many Jews already lived there. The state of Israel was created officially in May, 1948, but was immediately attacked by armies from the Arab countries of Jordan, Egypt, Lebanon, Syria and Iraq. The Israeli army fought off the attack, taking more land in the process. The rest of Palestine was

Above *On November 9, 1989, the Berlin Wall was brought crashing down by the people of Germany.*

TIMELINE
1979-1989

1979
Soviet invasion of Afghanistan. China subsequently decides to invade Vietnam.

1983
Reagan announces "Star Wars" Initiative.

1985
Mikhail Gorbachev becomes president of the Soviet Union and introduces many reforms.

1987
US and USSR sign treaty that bans short and medium range nuclear missiles in Europe.

1989
Revolutions in Czechoslovakia and Romania oust communist governments.

divided between Jordan and Egypt. In 1964, Arab governments set up the Palestine Liberation Organisation (PLO) to coordinate efforts against Israel. In 1967 Israel fought the Six-Day War against Arab states and by the end had nearly doubled the size of its territory. Tension in the Middle East was heightened. In 1973 Egypt and Syria launched fresh attacks on Israel in the Yom Kippur war. Conflict in the Middle East continues today.

COLD WAR THAW

In 1985 the Soviet Union's new leader, Mikhail Gorbachev, wanted to make his country more open and democratic and end the Cold War. However, it was the Eastern block countries themselves who brought about radical change. In East Germany and Czechoslovakia

peaceful protests saw an end to the communist regimes. Only in Romania was there widespread violence as forces loyal to the hated dictator Nicolae Ceausesce tried unsuccessfully to cling to power. One after another, Eastern European countries were freed from the domination of the Soviet Union. In November 1989 the Berlin Wall was opened. Thousands of East

Left *President Mikhail Gorbachev wanted a more peaceful Soviet Union.*

The state of Israel will be open to the immigration of Jews from all countries of their dispersion; will promote the development of the country for the benefit of all its inhabitants; will be based on the precepts of liberty, justice and peace taught by the Hebrew Prophets; will uphold the full social and political equality of all its citizens, without distinction of race, creed or sex; will guarantee full freedom of conscience, worship, education and culture; will safeguard the sanctity and inviolability of the shrines and Holy Places of all religions; and will dedicate itself to the principles of the Charter of the United Nations.

In the midst of wanton aggression, we yet call upon the Arab inhabitants of the State of Israel to return to the ways of peace and play their part in the development of the State, with full and equal citizenship and due representation in its bodies and institutions – provisional or permanent.

We offer peace and unity to all the neighbouring states and their peoples, and invite them to cooperate with the independent Jewish nation for the common good of all.

Declaration of the Independence of the State of Israel, *May 14, 1948.*

Above *A lone citizen stands in front of tanks on the Avenue of Eternal Peace in Beijing on June 5, 1989, during the crushing of the Tiananmen Square uprising.*

Far Right *Following the terrorist attacks of September 11th, 2001, United States planes were sent into Afghanistan to attack the Taliban government, accused of supporting the perpetrators of the attack.*

the protest with troops, killing hundreds of students between June 3 and 4.

REGIONS OF CONFLICT
In the Middle East, tension between Israel and its Arab neighbours continued. In 1987, a mass Palestinian uprising – or Intifada – was launched against the Israeli occupation, which continued until 1993. There was also conflict elsewhere in the region. In August 1990 Saddam Hussein, the leader of Iraq, invaded Kuwait. A coalition of armies led by the United States forced the Iraqis out of Kuwait.

NEW ENEMIES
The United States also suffered its worst ever terrorist attack. On September 11, 2001, four aircraft were hijacked and flown towards different targets in the United States. One crashed before it reached its target. Another hit the side of the Pentagon in Washington. Two planes hit the Twin Towers of the World Trade Center, which collapsed. More than three thousand people lost their lives.
As a result, the United States and other

Germans streamed into the west, and the East German government fell. By October 1990 the two parts of Germany were reunited. Soon, the Soviet Union was no more. The Cold War was over, but peaceful revolution was not universal and China was still controlled by communists. In 1989, students began a protest in Tiananmen Square, Beijing, calling for more freedom. The government crushed

"Today I was feeling in the walking mood and decided to walk outside. I am located in World Financial Center 1. To get to me you need to be on the 2nd floor of the Twin Towers to get on the internal bridge. But today I decided I would walk via the street.

About two minutes after I got out to the street I heard a loud explosion. I looked up and saw flames coming from the Twin Towers. I immediately thought it was a bomb. Debris was falling everywhere as if it were the ticket tape parade for the Yankees. Suddenly I was hit in the head. I do not think it was a piece of the plane, I thought it might be office supplies because paper was floating down. But what ever hit me hurt me. I just turned around and ran across the street."

Richard Wajda was on his way to work at the World Trade Center on September 11.

🎞 FILM EXCERPT 📁 GOVERNMENT DOCUMENT 🎤 INTERVIEW/BOOK EXTRACT 🎵 SONG EXCERPT

Above *Osama Bin Laden.*

Above *The blazing Twin Towers of the World Trade Center.*

TIMELINE 1989-2005

JUNE 3-4, 1989
Tiananmen Square revolt crushed.

NOV 9, 1989
Berlin Wall opened.

1990
Gorbachev awarded Nobel Peace Prize.

AUG 8 1990
Iraq invades Kuwait.

OCT 3 1990
Germany reunified.

DEC 26, 1991
Soviet Union dissolves.

SEPT 11, 2001
World Trade Center attack. US-led coalition later topples Taliban government in Afghanistan.

MAR 16, 2003
Attack on Iraq.

MAR 16, 2005
New parliament in Iraq opens.

countries began a "war on terror". The attack on the World Trade Center had been planned by a man called Osama Bin Laden, and it was believed that he was hiding in Afghanistan. When the Afghan government, which was controlled by a group called the Taliban, refused to give him up, the United States bombed the country until the government fell. The Americans and their allies then began to help Afghanistan become more democratic. In March 2003, the Americans again led an attack on Iraq because they believed that Saddam Hussein's government had weapons of mass destruction that it was planning to use against the rest of the world. Three weeks later Saddam Hussein's government collapsed.

"We know that Saddam Hussein is determined to keep his weapons of mass destruction; he's determined to make more. Given Saddam Hussein's history of aggression, given what we know of his grandiose plans, given what we know of his terrorist associations and given his determination to exact revenge on those who oppose him, should we take the risk that he will not some day use these weapons at a time and the place and in the manner of his choosing at a time when the world is in a much weaker position to respond? The United States will not and cannot run that risk to the American people. Leaving Saddam Hussein in possession of weapons of mass destruction for a few more months or years is not an option, not in a post-September 11th world."

US Secretary of State Colin Powell addresses the U.N. Security Council on February 5, 2003. Despite the US invasion of Iraq, no weapons of mass destruction have yet been found in Iraq.

CHAPTER 7

MAJOR FIGURES MEN OF THE WAR

The course of the Second World War was determined by the courage, sacrifice and determination of millions of people throughout the world. Both civilians and the military on both sides looked to their leaders for direction and as a source of inspiration. Political and military leaders had to fight a war and make sure that the ordinary needs of the people were also met.

ADOLF HITLER (1889-1945)

Adolf Hitler was the head of the Nazi Party and Chancellor (leader) of Germany from 1933 to 1945. He became dictator of Germany, built up his military strength and led the country into a war against Britain, France, the Soviet Union and the United States. For a time, his armies dominated much of Europe and North Africa. Eventually his actions resulted in defeat and ruin for Germany, the death of millions of people, including six million Jews killed by the Nazis, and the destruction and division of much of Europe. Adolf Hitler became involved in politics after World War I. He believed that Germans were part of a superior race because of the way they had descended, and that this race – the "Aryans" – should rule over "inferior" races including the Jews. He also believed that democracy was a threat to German strength.

EMPEROR HIROHITO (1901-1989)

Hirohito was the Emperor of Japan from 1926 until his death in 1989. After the atomic bombs fell on Hiroshima and Nagasaki he took action and demanded that the Japanese should surrender. After the war was over, he helped the Allies turn Japan into a democratic nation. He did this in 1946 by publicly denying his divine status. In the 1970s he toured the United States and Europe as a goodwill gesture. He died on January 7, 1989. His son became the new Emperor of Japan.

TOJO HIDEKI (1884-1948)

Tojo was the Prime Minister of Japan from 1941 until 1944. From 1935 he commanded the Japanese army as they fought the Chinese in Manchuria. In 1938 he returned to Tokyo and became part of Japan's military government. In 1940 he was made Minister of War. Two months before the attack on Pearl Harbour in 1941 he became Prime Minister of Japan. After the Allies occupied Japan he was arrested as a war criminal. He was executed on December 23, 1948.

JOSEPH STALIN (1879-1953)

Stalin's real name was Iosif Vissarionovich Dzhugashvili. He took the name Stalin, which means "Man of Steel", in 1910, after Lenin's death in 1924. Stalin became head of the Soviet Union. He remained in power for 24 years. During that time he ruled by terror and millions of people died because of his actions. Stalin took personal control of the armed forces during the Second World War and appealed to the Soviet people to fight against the Germans. As the war came to end Stalin was determined that his country would never be threatened again. He made sure that friendly communist-led governments were installed throughout Eastern Europe. His mistrust of Western Europe and the Americans helped to start the Cold War. Stalin died on March 5, 1953.

FIELD MARSHAL ERWIN ROMMEL (1891-1944)

Field Marshal Rommel was the best-known German military commander. At the start of the Second World War he was in command of a tank division that pushed British and French troops back to the English Channel. As a reward for this he was made a lieutenant general and given command of the Afrika Korps, the German soldiers based in North Africa. After victory at the Battle of Grazala in 1942, Rommel was promoted to field marshal and earned the nickname of 'Desert Fox'. Rommel was given command of the German defences in northern France and had to face the Allied assault on D-Day. In July 1944 Rommel had a minor part in a plot to kill Hitler. The plot failed. Rommel was given the choice of standing trial or suicide. He chose to take his own life.

GENERAL GEORGY ZHUKOV (1896-1974)

Zhukov led the Soviet army to final victory over the Germans with the occupation of Berlin. Zhukov became more and more powerful when he was put in charge of the defence of Moscow against the invading German army. When the threat to Moscow was lifted he began to push the Germans back. He led the final assault on Berlin in 1945 and then remained in Germany to lead the Soviet occupation of the eastern part of Germany. He returned in triumph to the Soviet Union in 1946. Stalin was jealous of his popularity and so he demoted him and sent him away from Moscow. After Stalin died in 1953 Zhukov returned to Moscow, was made deputy leader of the ministry of defence and became a leading member of the ruling Communist Party. He died in 1974.

WINSTON CHURCHILL (1874-1965)

Winston Churchill was Prime Minister of Britain twice. From the late 1920s he was a critic of the official policy of appeasement towards Hitler and he found himself out of favour in the Conservative party. With the outbreak of war, however, he returned to government and soon became Prime Minister. During the rest of the war Churchill became best known for his stirring speeches. In the summer of 1945 the Labour Party defeated the Conservative Party and Churchill was no longer Prime Minister. He won the 1951 election, however, and served as Prime Minister for four years. He died ten years later in January 1965.

FRANKLIN ROOSEVELT (1882-1945)

Franklin Roosevelt was elected President of the United States in 1933. He was elected during the Depression, offering a "New Deal" to put people back to work. At the start of the Second World War he kept America neutral. However, Roosevelt saw that Britain needed help fighting Nazi Germany. Congress passed his "Lend-Lease" laws that gave practical help to the British. Roosevelt brought America into the Second World War after the Japanese attack on Pearl Harbour. In January 1943 he agreed with Churchill that the only option for Germany and Japan was unconditional surrender. Roosevelt died on April 12, 1945. His funeral train was watched by millions of Americans.

HARRY S TRUMAN (1884-1972)

Harry Truman became President of the United States in 1945 after the death of Franklin Roosevelt. It was Truman that decided to use the two atomic bombs on Japanese cities and took the American people to victory over Germany and Japan. He also took America into the Cold War with the Soviet Union. His suspicions led to the "Truman Doctrine". This was designed to contain the expansion of Soviet power around the world. Truman did this mainly through the Marshall Plan and the creation of NATO in 1949. He also sent troops to fight communists in Korea and provided help in the fight against Vietnamese communists. Truman retired in 1952 and died twenty years later.

ADMIRAL CHESTER WILLIAM NIMITZ (1885-1966)

Admiral Nimitz served alongside General MacArthur in leading the Allied war on Japan in Asia and the Pacific. He served in the First World War as a submarine commander in the Atlantic. During the 1930s he rose through the ranks of the American Navy. In December 1941, after the Japanese attack on Pearl Harbour, he was appointed Commander in Chief of the American Pacific fleet. He was known as a great military thinker who was willing to take risks, like at the Battle of Midway. The great success of the American Navy in the Pacific was due largely to his leadership. He retired from the Navy in 1947 and died in 1966.

DWIGHT EISENHOWER (1890-1969)

In 1942 General Eisenhower was made head of American forces in Europe. By December 1944 he controlled a military force in Europe of over four million. As the Cold War with the Soviet Union began he was made commander of the North Atlantic Treaty Organisation (NATO). In 1953 he was persuaded to run for President of the United States. His huge popularity amongst the American people meant that he was easily elected. He remained President until 1961. Under his presidency the war in Korea came to an end. Eisenhower was known as an opponent of the Soviet Union but he also tried to have good relations with the Soviet leadership. He died in 1969.

GENERAL DOUGLAS MACARTHUR (1880-1964)

General MacArthur commanded Allied troops in the Pacific and Asia. Under his command the Philippines was invaded and conquered by the Japanese. MacArthur retreated to Australia. With Admiral Nimitz he led a combined American and Australian force that gradually took islands in the Pacific that had been taken by the Japanese. With the surrender of Japan in September 1945 he was put in charge of the reconstruction of Japan. He helped in creating a democratic government and made sure that Japan would never be a military power again. In June 1950, he headed a United Nations army in South Korea that was fighting off an invasion from North Korea. He died in April 1964.

GLOSSARY

alliance being joined together to cooperate for a common purpose.

appeasement submissive behaviour in the hope of bringing about peace.

astronaut a person who travels in space.

Atlantic an ocean that separates America from Europe and Africa.

atomic relating to atoms; an atomic bomb is powered by the splitting of atoms.

Allied Powers The nations, primarily Britain, France, the Soviet Union and the United States, allied against the Axis powers.

Axis Powers The countries opposed to the Allies, led by Germany, Italy and Japan.

Battle of the Bulge a campaign of World War II fought in the Ardennes area of France.

Battle of Britain name given to the struggle for supremacy in the air that took place over southern England in 1940-41 between the British and German air forces.

Berlin Wall a barrier erected across the centre of Berlin to prevent people in Soviet-held East Germany escaping to West Germany.

Blitz attack or bombing from the air, especially that which took place over Britain during World War II.

blitzkrieg lightning war, an intense burst of bombing.

broadcast a radio or TV programme; to transmit material by radio or TV for reception to the public.

civil war war between citizens of the same state.

civilian a person who is not a member of the armed forces.

coalition a combination or alliance formed for a specific purpose.

Cold War name given to hostile relations between America and the Soviet Union, and their respective allies, which did not involve actual combat.

communism a social theory under which society should be classless, private property abolished, and factories and land collectively owned.

concentration camp a prison camp for people whom the authorities wish to remove or segregate from society.

D-Day June 6, 1944; the first day of the Allied invasion of Europe in World War II.

democracy a form of government in which power is vested in the people and is administered by them or by their elected representatives.

Depression a period of massive economic slump, especially during the 1930s (also known as the Great Depression).

guerrilla a member of a force that engages in warfare or harassment of an army, usually operating in small groups.

hijack to steal something while it is in transit.

Holocaust term given to the extermination of six million Jews by the Nazis.

independent not relying on or being dependent on others.

Intifada the uprising in 1987, and continued resistance from Palestine to Israeli occupation of the Gaza Strip and the West Bank of the River Jordan.

Iwo Jima an island in the Pacific.

Lend-Lease Act an arrangement by which America agreed to supply weapons to countries fighting the Axis.

Lebensraum Nazi policy which translates as "Living space", advocating taking over land in other European countries to increase German territory.

Nazi a member of an extreme political party in Germany, the National Socialists.

negotiate discuss with the aim of reaching mutual agreement.

Netherlands a kingdom in western Europe, divided into provinces, one of which is Holland.

Pacific The ocean between Asia and America.

PLO Palestine Liberation Organisation, a group set up to fight Israel's occupation of Palestine. Originally a terrorist group, it renounced terrorism in 1988.

Taliban a group which ruled Afghanistan until defeated by the United States after the terrorist attack on the World Trade Center.

Pearl Harbour A naval base in Hawaii which the Japanese attacked without warning on December 7, 1941. Much of the US Pacific fleet was destroyed and the incident led to the US entering World War II.

Propaganda information spread to influence people for or against a particular policy or idea.

Soviet Union also known as the Union of Soviet Socialist Republics (USSR). Countries formerly under communist rule: Albania, Armenia, Azerbaijan, Belarus, Bosnia and Herzegovina, Bulgaria, Croatia, Czech Republic, Estonia, Georgia, Hungary, Kazakhstan, Kyrgyz Republic, Latvia, Lithuania, Macedonia, Moldova, Mongolia, Montenegro, Poland, Romania, Russia, Serbia, Slovakia, Slovenia, Tajikistan, Turkmenistan, Ukraine and Uzbekistan.

Surrender to give up something, especially when forced.

VE Day Victory in Europe, the official end of World War II in Europe.

Velvet Revolution a term applied to a revolution that was achieved without bloodshed, especially the revolution in Czechoslovakia.

VJ Day Victory over Japan Day, the official end of World War II in Japan.

INDEX

ACKNOWLEDGEMENTS

PICTURE CREDITS:

Every effort has been made to trace the copyright holders, and we apologise
in advance for any unintentional omissions. We would be pleased to
insert the appropriate acknowledgements in any subsequent edition
of this publication.

B=bottom; C=centre; L=left; R=right; T=top

Aviation Photographs: 4-5c, 24t, 25c, 28b.
Corbis: 5b, 7b, 9cr, 12, 11t, 12-13 all, 18b, 23cr, 28t, 29cr, 34b, 36 all,
38t, 39 all, Everett Collection: 6-7c, 32c.
Library of Congress: 8b, 16t, 18b, 19b, 24b, 28t.